RESETTLING IN PLACE

A Vietnamese American Catholic Experience

Committee on Cultural Diversity in the Church
Subcommittee on Asian and Pacific Island Affairs
United States Conference of Catholic Bishops
Washington, DC

Resettling in Place: A Vietnamese American Catholic Experience was developed by the Subcommittee on Asian and Pacific Island Affairs of the United States Conference of Catholic Bishops (USCCB). It was reviewed and approved by the Committee on Cultural Diversity in the Church chairman, Bishop Daniel E. Flores and authorized for publication by the Administrative Committee. It has been directed for publication by the undersigned.

Msgr. Ronny E. Jenkins
General Secretary, USCCB

Cover image: *Apparition of Our Lady of La Vang*. (2008, Angelo Gherardi, St. Jude Liturgical Design.) Chapel of Our Lady of La Vang, Vietnam. © Basilica of the National Shrine of the Immaculate Conception, Washington, D.C. Photographer: Geraldine M. Rohling.

First printing, November 2015
Second printing, February 2018

ISBN 978-1-60137-480-6

Contents

Foreword

RESETTLING IN PLACE: A VIETNAMESE AMERICAN CATHOLIC EXPERIENCE

In 2011, the Subcommittee on Asian and Pacific Island Affairs (SCAPA) celebrated the tenth anniversary of the statement of the United States Conference of Catholic Bishops (USCCB), Asian and Pacific Presence: Harmony in Faith. As part of this celebration, SCAPA commissioned writers for a series of small books to inform clergy, ministers, and parishioners of the Catholicism of Asian and Pacific Island communities. Rev. Linh N. Hoang, OFM, associate professor of religious studies with expertise in historical theology and Asian religions in America, graciously accepted the task of writing on the Vietnamese American experience.

The Vietnamese American experience is symbolic of Christ's Paschal Mystery. Like Jesus' Way of the Cross to Calvary, Vietnamese Catholics journeyed through tides of persecution and years of displacement as refugees to the United States. Despite many trials, the Vietnamese people have held on to their faith and brought it with them. Their faith, characterized by hope rooted in culture, expressed in their mother tongue (and in English), has facilitated not only their adaptation to their new homeland but also their growth. The rate of growth of the number of Catholics in the United States has been higher than the rate of growth of the number of Catholics in Vietnam. The number of vocations to the priesthood and religious life has been significant and is a distinctive contribution to the Church in the United States. These religious vocations, augmented by a steady stream of lay leadership serving in all aspects of pastoral ministry, have gained them recognition within the Church in the United States. Still, the seed of faith continues to be sown in Vietnamese households as many parents motivate their children to consider Eucharistic spirituality and encourage participation in the Vietnamese Eucharistic Youth Movement.

Having this small book published in the name of the SCAPA is a symbol of appreciation from the Church in the United States for the Vietnamese people and for their relentless participation in the Church's work of evangelization and the New Evangelization. The subcommittee is grateful to Fr. Hoang for his work on this book. *Resettling in Place* delivers a message of Christian faith and hope to Vietnamese as well as to those whose lives are marked by persecution or maimed by hardship of any kind.

Most Rev. Randolph R. Calvo
Bishop of Reno
Chairman of the Subcommittee on Asia and Pacific Island Affairs
United States Conference of Catholic Bishops

Introduction

Vietnamese American Catholics are relatively new to the religious landscape of the United States. In 1975, many Vietnamese fled their war-torn country and resettled in various parts of the world, with a large number accepted into the United States of America. The first wave of refugees numbered about 130,000, and the flights of refugees out of Vietnam continued into the first half of the 1990s.[1] Among the large influx of Vietnamese refugees, there was a disproportionately large number of Catholics. By the mid-1990s, about 30 percent of Vietnamese in America were Catholic, and by the 2010 U.S. Census, that number had grown to approximately 489,000, again making up 30 percent of a total population of approximately 1.6 million Vietnamese in the United States.[2] By contrast, in Vietnam, Catholics make up only about 7 percent of the overall population. Many factors contribute to this disproportionate representation, but a major reason is the years of religious persecution that Catholics, as well as other religious followers, such as Buddhists, endured in Vietnam. As Vietnamese Catholics resettled, their faith played a major role in establishing their place in America. They combined a deeply spiritual and devotional practice of Catholicism with their traditional cultural practices. This religious and cultural melding, combined with years of persecution, garnered Vietnamese American Catholics a distinctive place within the American Catholic Church.

This portrait of Vietnamese American Catholics is divided into four sections. The first section describes how Catholicism historically took root in Vietnam over three hundred years ago, highlighting the colonial influence as well as the civil and political turmoil. The second section considers the way Vietnamese Catholic refugees and immigrants utilized their faith to adapt in America, giving attention

---

1 Jeremy Hein, *From Vietnam, Laos, and Cambodia: A Refugee Experience in the United States* (New York: Twayne Publishers, 1995), 35-37.

2 Elizabeth M. Hoeffel, Sonya Rastogi, Myoung Ouk Kim, and Hasan Shahid, "The Asian Population: 2010," *2010 Census Briefs* (The United States Census Bureau, 2012), 3-4.

to their unique contributions. The third section describes the characteristics unique to Vietnamese American Catholics. The conclusion draws attention to the hopes and concerns of the community in order to address the pastoral needs to sustain the future participation of the Vietnamese American Catholic community within the larger American Catholic Church.

History of Vietnamese Catholicism

UNDER COLONIALISM

In the seventeenth century, Vietnam had cast off the one thousand plus years of sporadic occupation by the Chinese and had found relative independence. It still maintained an imperial system similar to China's. European countries at this time were expanding their exploration of foreign lands and claiming new territories. In particular, France, a very wealthy and powerful Roman Catholic nation, sent many explorers and missionaries to all parts of the world through the *Société des Missions-Étrangères* (Foreign Mission Society, MEP). French Jesuits came to Vietnam in 1615. They encountered people at the time who practiced different native spiritual beliefs and other religious traditions such as Buddhism, Taoism, and Confucianism. Alexandre de Rhodes, a French Jesuit, was instrumental in establishing a formidable French Catholic presence in Vietnam. In 1624, he landed in the southern province of Vietnam known as Cochinchina and then traveled to the central region of Annam and the northern kingdom of Tonkin in 1627. Through the collective hard work of his fellow Jesuits, de Rhodes used a newly adapted Romanized Vietnamese script of Catholic texts to teach thousands of people.[3] This script was later adopted throughout each region of Vietnam and called *quoc ngu* (national language). Gradually, *quoc ngu* almost entirely replaced the Chinese characters that were traditionally used in Vietnamese writing. The Jesuits' invention became the country's standard form of writing. Thus, the very beginning of Catholic contact in Vietnam contributed to one of the core expressions of Vietnamese culture, that of its national script.

In the seventeenth and eighteenth centuries, missionaries worked tirelessly throughout the three provinces of Vietnam. It was

---

3   Peter C. Phan, *Mission and Catechesis: Alexandre de Rhodes and Inculturation in Seventeenth-Century Vietnam* (Maryknoll, NY: Orbis Books, 1998), 88-90.

a politically tumultuous period, as different imperial families fought for full control of the country. The Nguyen ruled over the southern kingdom of Cochinchina, and the Trinh family held power over the northern Tonkin region. The Trinh disliked Catholics and instituted laws in 1625 that prohibited any Catholic worship or evangelization. Anyone could be persecuted for violating any aspect of the laws. Under a succession of different emperors, more laws and edicts were implemented to suppress the growing Catholic population.[4] This did not deter the missionaries or their new converts, who paid great respect to the missionaries, even to the extent of pledging to die with them. As a consequence, martyrdom became a profound historical feature of Vietnamese Catholicism. These martyrs stand as a witness to the faith for Vietnamese Catholics today. This will be discussed further in the fourth section.

In 1788, a peasant rebellion known as Tay Son unified the country under the rebel leader who had proclaimed himself sole emperor. This uprising caused the only surviving heir of the Nguyen family, Nguyen Anh, to seek the assistance of France with the help of Msgr. Pierre Pigneau de Behaine, who convinced the French King Louis XVI to provide military support. The Tay Son rebels, concerned that Catholics would support the Nguyen emperor, issued an anti-Catholic edict and approved persecution against the missionaries and Vietnamese Catholics.[5]

With French backing, Nguyen Anh suppressed the rebels and ultimately took control of all regions of Vietnam by 1802. He declared himself emperor and took the imperial name of Gia Long. He initiated a policy of religious tolerance, which would only last until 1820, when his son Minh Mang inherited the throne. Minh Mang revived Confucianism and the Chinese model of ruling to reestablish order in the country. He believed that Catholics instigated chaos among the people and constituted a great threat to his rule. Thus, he ordered a

---

4   *Mission and Catechesis*, 54-55.
5   Phan Phat Huon, *History of the Catholic Church in Vietnam* (Long Beach, CA: Cuu The Tung Thu, 2000), 310-312.

suppression of Catholic practices in 1825. The missionaries, however, continued to be active in defiance of the imperial prohibition against Catholics.[6] By their example, the missionaries encouraged new converts to attend to daily worship and practice the faith. This will became an enduring factor for Vietnamese Catholics as they strongly embraced their faith, despite great opposition and persecution.

Anti-Catholic activities intensified under the Emperor Tu-Duc, who ruled from 1847 to 1883. The emperor was deeply suspicious of French intentions in Vietnam, and he saw Vietnamese Catholics as part of the French strategy to colonize the whole country. The French Emperor Napoleon III took up the cause of Catholics in Vietnam and used their persecution as a reason for invading the country and seizing Saigon, including the three surrounding provinces, in 1859. Emperor Tu-Duc, preoccupied with suppressing a northern uprising, was not able to defend the south. In 1862, he ceded the southern region to France and agreed to the establishment of a French protectorate. Then, in the 1880s, after France defeated China, which claimed its ancient sovereignty over Vietnam, the French extended control over all of Vietnam. They established the southern region directly as a colony and the central and northern regions as protectorates.[7] This was the first time that a European country controlled all of Vietnam, and it initiated approximately one hundred years of French colonization.

During this French colonial period, Vietnamese Catholics were frequently seen as agents of a foreign power by nationalistic Vietnamese. Their suspicion effectively limited any cooperation among the entire Vietnamese people, even though many Catholics were still nationalistic and opposed French occupation. They were also generally against any political machinations, especially the disturbing rise of Communism. One of the first Catholic publications in Vietnam to address Communism was a 1927 booklet, *The Question*

---

6   *History of the Catholic Church in Vietnam*, 320-323.
7   *History of the Catholic Church in Vietnam*, 324.

of Communism, which attacked Communists as godless and violent.[8] Communists and many other leftists tended to be antagonistic toward Catholicism, which led to a continual feeling of unease for Catholics, causing many to move to other parts of the country. This first internal migration was mostly from north to south, but there were southern Communist sympathizers who migrated to the north. Catholics had created tight-knit communities, aiding in a smooth migration from one place to another. They organized strategically in various parts of the migration route to assist in the journey. This experience would be instrumental when migration occurred again in the country in 1954, and then across international borders in 1975. For Vietnamese Catholics, the uprooting and resettling have been part of the colonial and twentieth-century experience that prepared many who fled to the United States.

In the mid-twentieth century, as the Second World War raged, Vietnam was not immune to its violent effects. Japan had invaded and then occupied the country in early 1942. By August 1945, when Japan surrendered, the Communist-dominated nationalist forces known as the Viet Minh found themselves the only strong internal power in Vietnam. The last of the French-controlled Vietnamese emperors, Bao-dai, abdicated, and Ho Chi Minh declared the independence of Vietnam, now known as the Democratic Republic of Vietnam, on September 2, 1945. Japanese forces remained in Vietnam, and the Allies moved in to disarm them and send them back to their own country. The Allies were able to employ China, still under the Nationalist government of Chiang Kai-chek, to disarm the Japanese in northern Vietnam, and Britain was assigned the south. While the Chinese allowed the Viet Minh to maintain control over Hanoi and the north, the British helped the French seize control of the south and reestablish French colonial power. After the British and Chinese left in 1946, Vietnam was divided into north and south once again.[9]

---

8   Charles Keith, *Catholic Vietnam: A Church from Empire to Nation* (Berkeley, Los Angeles & London: University of California Press, 2012), 126.

9   William J. Duiker, *Ho Chi Minh: A Life* (New York: Hyperion, 2000), 20-22.

The French and the new Vietnamese government accepted one another uneasily. In March 1946, Ho Chi Minh signed an agreement with France in which he accepted the deployment of French troops in the north in return for recognition of the Democratic Republic of Vietnam.[10] France was not interested in seeing a truly independent Vietnam, and the Viet Minh had no desire to see the country continue under French colonial rule.

In early 1947, tensions between the two sides erupted into armed fighting, and the first Vietnam War began. In the early 1950s, the growing army of the Democratic Republic of Vietnam, under the command of General Vo Nguyen Giap, began a series of offenses against the French, achieving a victory at the city of Dien Bien Phu in May 1954. This outcome prompted an international conference on Vietnam in Geneva, Switzerland, to recognize a temporary division of the country into North and South. In the North, the Communist-led Democratic Republic of Vietnam ruled from Hanoi. In the South, the Republic of Vietnam, under the French-supported Emperor Bao-dai, ruled from Saigon, with Ngo Dinh Diem, who was a Catholic, as the premier. This divided the people, who took sides between the political parties. There was a strong crackdown on religious people, especially Catholics and Buddhists. Unlike the first internal migration, which involved mainly Catholics, this division of the country caused other religious people to seek safe places. Some South Vietnamese who sympathized with Ho Chi Minh's government moved north.[11] Likewise, about one million northerners, including six hundred thousand to eight hundred thousand Catholics as well as Buddhists, fled south on U.S. and French aircraft and naval vessels. As with the early migration, Catholics were instrumental in assisting one another in their journey. In many cases, the Catholic refugees of the 1954 division fled as entire villages, so that northern Catholic villages were reconstituted in the south.

---

10   *Ho Chi Minh: A Life*, 355-357.
11   *Ho Chi Minh: A Life*, 67-69.

CATHOLICS UNDER CIVIL UNREST

During this period of civil unrest, Catholics continued to strengthen their own sense of faith and national identity. Many Catholic programs and groups were formed to instruct the younger generation. Catholic associations brought together boys and girls aged six to eighteen to engage in many activities ranging from worship, contemplation, and evangelizing to physical exercise, outdoor activities, games, retreat days, and charity work. Members were expected to attend weekly meetings, annual conferences, and other activities, all in club uniforms. Most associations had some sort of a recreation hall for study and activities, often on the grounds of a church. Although many groups, such as Catholic Boy Scouts, focused mainly on social and community life, others, such as Catholic Youth and Eucharistic Crusades, made strict religious demands of their members. They were asked to pray regularly, saying an Our Father, Hail Mary, and Glory Be every day for the health of their association and for the conversion of sinners and nonbelievers. Members of nearly all youth associations were required to attend Mass, receive Communion regularly, go to confession, and participate in religious festivals. Evangelizing was an important activity of most Catholic youth associations; their members regularly accompanied members of the clergy seeking converts and handed out religious tracts.[12] Some of these groups have been reestablished in places where Vietnamese have resettled, including the United States.

Besides activities for the young people, Vietnamese Catholics also organized gatherings and groups for the adults that kept them apace with the Universal Catholic Church. These would bring people together for spiritual and religious formation as well as to update them on what was happening with the political unrest in the country. Papal Days and worldwide Marian apparitions became part of Catholic life in Vietnam. Papal Days would honor the current pope but also other popes who were receptive to the Vietnamese Catholics. These days

---

12   *Catholic Vietnam*, 130-131.

would entail a Mass followed by a communal celebration of a festive meal. There was also a great devotion to the Blessed Mother Mary. The belief in the apparitions of Mary in Vietnam motivated many Catholics to continue to pray and honor Mary in a very public manner. The faithful began to see their connection to a Universal Church that could help their own formation and aid them in their plight in an oppressive civil conflict. Eucharistic congresses began to be held regularly in the late twentieth century, first in France and then worldwide. They were organized to deepen devotion to the Eucharist by gathering Catholic communities together in Holy Communion and the Mass.[13] For the first time, the Vietnamese Catholic Church witnessed these large gatherings of Catholics, which had not yet been seen in Vietnam. It was the first time that large numbers of Catholics were able to freely express their faith. This strong dedication to the Eucharist would instill in Vietnamese Catholics a strong presence of Christ in their lives and lead to a devotional practice that would mobilize Vietnamese Catholics in America.

It should be noted that Catholic worship was primarily oral, with prayers, songs, and stories transmitted through homilies during Mass or in catechism classes. Texts circulated primarily among the clergy and elites. The rise of *quoc ngu* in Catholic life during the early nineteenth century did improve literacy rates and contribute to better lay participation. Nevertheless, printed material was still marginally present in the lives of many Catholics well into the twentieth century.[14]

THE FALL OF SAIGON

Returning to the historical narrative, in 1955, Diem organized and had won elections that forced Bao-dai to abdicate, and Diem declared himself president of Vietnam. He refused to take part in elections for national reunification of the country. This refusal, along with his Catholic background, caused opposition against Diem's presidency.

13   *Catholic Vietnam,* 173-176.
14   *Catholic Vietnam,* 125-131.

The Communist North Vietnam continued to organize its power with those disaffected by Diem. This caused great concern for the United States, which was already wary about the rise of Communism in the region. In 1963, a military coup overthrew Diem. The new leader of South Vietnam proved unable to maintain control, and by 1965, U.S. President Lyndon B. Johnson sent in ground troops. It must be noted that the participation of the United States was in negotiation for years, especially as the French realized that they could not handle the complicated situation by themselves.

Although military and political leaders believed they were winning the war, by 1968, the North Vietnamese troops launched the Tet Offensive, which changed the course of the war. In 1973, the Paris peace talks ended with the United States agreeing on a timetable for withdrawing troops and turning the war over to the South Vietnamese army. The South was not prepared; thus, in April 1975, Saigon fell to an invasion of North Vietnamese troops. It was a mixed reception, with some Vietnamese welcoming the Northerners and others horrified at the prospect of being under Communist rule. Thus began one of the largest flights of refugees across international borders that the world had ever witnessed.

Since Catholics had been disproportionately involved in supporting the South Vietnamese government in opposition to Communism, they often suffered at the hands of the new authorities. Catholics would be heavily represented among the refugees fleeing Vietnam, contributing to the presence of Vietnamese Catholics in different parts of the world, especially in the United States.

Vietnamese Catholics in America

In the latter part of 1975, the U.S. government, faced with the challenge of resettling thousands of Vietnamese refugees, initiated an orderly resettlement plan. The government resettled refugees by distributing them evenly throughout the fifty states so that no one state would absorb the full financial responsibility. The initial refugee asylum seekers in the United States became known as the first-wave refugees. The flight of Vietnamese refugees is often characterized as a series of waves. There were five waves of refugee movements from 1975 to the mid-1990s. Each wave was distinctive, based on the professional and educational backgrounds of the people as well as their struggles to leave Vietnam. Those who arrived in this first wave were a mixed group of people but predominantly professionals and those who had direct contact with American military personnel and civil servants. It contained a large Catholic population compared to the four subsequent waves.[15]

The early attempts by the U.S. government to settle refugees around the nation led Vietnamese to live in midwestern and mountain states least populated by recent immigrants; however, through secondary migration, distinctive Vietnamese enclaves emerged. In 1980, over one-fifth of the Vietnamese in America lived in California, and over one-third were concentrated in nine states: Texas, Louisiana, Georgia, Massachusetts, Illinois, Michigan, Oregon, Pennsylvania, and Washington. By 1990, almost half of the Vietnamese in America had settled or relocated in California, and one-third of the rapidly growing population was clustered in major metropolitan areas as well as coastal regions. Vietnamese tended to move out of the central regions of the United States to the far West, far South, and Northeast.

---

15   James M. Freeman, *Changing Identities: Vietnamese Americans 1975-1995* (Boston: Allyn and Bacon, 1995), 23-25.

FORMING FAITH ORGANIZATIONS

Vietnamese Catholics took up strategies learned from their home country: creating tight-knit communities, establishing faith organizations, and networking in order to migrate smoothly. One of the first small communities of Vietnamese Catholics was established in east New Orleans in 1975 right after the resettlement process. It eventually formed into a parish called Mary Queen of Vietnam Catholic Church, which has now grown to be one of the largest Vietnamese parishes in the United States, with a mission extension into another part of the city of New Orleans.[16] Also in 1975, another group of Vietnamese Catholics initiated a small gathering of twenty-five Catholic families in Virginia. They have now grown to be the first official national parish, which is now called the Holy Martyrs of Vietnam Catholic Church in Arlington, Virginia. The designation as a national parish took place in 1979, only four years after the refugee flight out of Vietnam, and is unique because national parishes are not easily granted status by Church law. The community has also distinguished itself as a national parish for all Vietnamese Catholics. They boast attendance and support from Vietnamese living across the United States.[17]

Many dioceses in the United States have responded to the pastoral needs of the Vietnamese by creating national parishes, of which there are now well over forty. There are also well over 150 parishes across the United States that provide Vietnamese-language Masses. Some of these parishes have reestablished organizations that they formed in Vietnam (described earlier), especially youth organizations such as Eucharistic Youth Movement and the Boy Scouts.

In August 1978, the Congregation of the Mother Co-Redemptrix (CMC) in Carthage, Missouri, hosted the first Marian Days. These are pilgrimage days for Vietnamese refugees who resettled in the United States and wish to give thanks to God through Mary, celebrating her Assumption on August 15. The CMC is a vowed religious community

---

16   Carl L. Bankston III, "Vietnamese-American Catholicism: Transplanted and Flourishing," *Catholic Historian* 18:1 (Winter, 2000: 36-53), 46.

17   Holy Martyrs of Vietnam Catholic Church, *www.cttdva.com*.

of men who fled in 1975 and resettled in Missouri. The bishop of the Diocese of Springfield–Cape Girardeau, Missouri, at that time was Bernard Law, who gave land and buildings that previously housed the Oblates of Mary Immaculate (OMI) in Carthage to the CMC to establish their community. Their first Marian Days brought together about five hundred Vietnamese families from across the United States. This has grown into an annual Vietnamese Catholic gathering that attracts Vietnamese from all over the United States and around the world. Since the mid-1980s, this pilgrimage has ballooned to over sixty thousand people annually. The pilgrimage has grown into a time for family and friends to reunite and give thanks for their faith in God. It also provides a time for those who are not Catholic to reunite with other Vietnamese to remember the events that changed their lives and the history of their homeland.

As discussed previously, Vietnamese Catholics continue to form networks and organizations across their newfound place in the United States. For instance, the Vietnamese Catholic Community of Clergy and Religious was founded in 1978, and at the first convention of Vietnamese Catholics in 1980, the Vietnamese Catholic Federation was created, which brought the clergy and religious under the same federation. The first president elected was Fr. Joseph Tinh. In addition to a federation for religious and priests, Vietnamese Catholics were also concerned with creating organizations for their lay brothers and sisters. Thus, the National Pastoral Center for Vietnamese Apostolate was established in 1989, with Fr. Dominic Luong as the first director, who would later become the first Vietnamese American bishop. In 2003, three Asian American priests were ordained to become the first Asian American bishops of any dioceses in the United States. Bishop Dominic Luong, Bishop Oscar Solis, and Bishop Ignatius Wang were all ordained for dioceses in California. Bishop Luong was assigned as auxiliary bishop of the Diocese of Orange County. Bishop Solis was assigned to the Archdiocese of Los Angeles and Bishop Wang to the Archdiocese of San Francisco. Bishop Luong continues to be a strong advocate and voice for Vietnamese Catholics in America. His involvement from the beginning of their presence speaks to his leadership and continual encouragement of leaders among the ranks of the Vietnamese Catholic community.

In 1993, the Vietnamese Catholic Congress—a gathering of clergy, religious, and laity—was organized, establishing meetings every other year under the sponsorship of the National Pastoral Center for the Vietnamese Apostolate and the Federation of Vietnamese Catholics in collaboration with the Office for the Pastoral Care of Migrants and Refugees of the United States Conference of Catholic Bishops. The goal of the Congress has been to establish plans and goals for Vietnamese Catholic communities throughout the United States.

SUPPORTING VOCATIONS

Vietnamese Catholics are traditionally supportive of encouraging vocations and forming future leaders for the Church. Vocations to the priesthood and religious life are among the highest of any ethnic group in the American Catholic Church. According to the *Lien Doan Cong Giao Viet Nam Tai Hoa Ky* (Federation of Vietnamese Catholics in the USA), there are approximately 750 priests, both secular and religious, serving dioceses in the United States; well over 65 permanent deacons; 500 perpetually professed sisters; and 350 sisters in temporary vows.[18] There are fifty religious orders or societies that have Vietnamese American vocations. Religious societies with large Vietnamese membership include the Society of the Divine Word (SVD) and the Society of Jesus (SJ). Moreover, the Center for Applied Research in the Apostolate (CARA) supports the fact that the overall Asian and Pacific Islander (API) priests and religious overrepresent relative to their proportion of the U.S. adult Catholic population. Even though CARA does not have the specific number for Vietnamese,

---

18   According to the Federation of Vietnamese Catholics in the USA, the list of priests, religious, and deacons is not complete, but they have made a concerted effort to collect as many names as possible and validate those with the official lists of dioceses and religious orders. At the time of this article, it is the most up-to-date list (see *www.liendoanconggiao.net*).

their data indicate that priestly vocations among foreign-born Asians and Pacific Islanders are quite healthy and continue to be steady.[19]

There are many different factors in the vocational commitment among Vietnamese Catholics. These include family support, the parish community, and the larger Vietnamese Catholic networks. The family's strong filial piety, as stated previously, is instrumental in planting the seed of faith in young people. They are the first encounter of vocations for the young.

Another major factor is the networks and organizations that have sprouted up among the Vietnamese Catholics. One organization needs mentioning, because it has influenced a high number of religious and priestly vocations. The Vietnamese Eucharistic Youth Movement is a volunteer faith organization that helps teach young people about the basics of their Catholic faith as well as nurture them to live exemplary Christian lives. This organization is connected to an international Church movement for the formation of children ages five to twenty-five. It is the junior branch of the Apostleship of Prayer.[20] The Vietnamese Eucharistic Youth Movement is distinctive because of its attention to the language and culture of Vietnam in its formation of children and young people in the United States. Also, it is unique in that adults volunteer their time to help in passing on the faith to the young people. This organization now has chapters across many different dioceses in the United States. It boasts over 15,000 members in seventy Vietnamese Catholic communities and parishes under the direction of 1,300 volunteer coordinating-leaders and chaplains.[21] They also regularly attend World Youth Day celebrations.

This brief historical description of the plight and resettlement to America of Vietnamese Catholics highlights their struggles and

---

19 See *http://cara.georgetown.edu/*, specifically the studies on Religious Vocation and Priestly Ordinations in the United States. See also Mary L. Gautier, Paul M. Perl, and Stephen J. Fichter, *Same Call, Different Men: The Evolution of the Priesthood Since Vatican II* (Collegeville, MN: Liturgical Press, 2012).

20 See *www.apostleshipofprayer.net/eym/what-is-EYM-en.aspx*.

21 "The Vietnamese Eucharistic Youth Movement History," *http://tntt-toronto.ca/index.php?view=article&catid=1%3AGioi_Thieu&id=21%3Atntt-hostory-english&format=pdf&option=com_content&Itemid=2*, 1. Please also see *http://www.tntt.org/*.

successes. The following section addresses some of the characteristics that define why Vietnamese Catholics are strong in their resolve and determined in their faith.

Three Characteristics of Vietnamese American Catholicism

Three characteristics of Vietnamese American Catholicism ground it in the broader Catholic tradition as well as create a unique Vietnamese contribution to the Church Universal: ancestor veneration as part of filial piety, a deep Marian devotion, and martyrdom.

ANCESTOR VENERATION AND FILIAL PIETY

The practice of ancestor veneration is deeply rooted in the larger Vietnamese culture and continues to strongly influence Vietnamese Catholics. Ancestor veneration involves the practice of living family members doing what they can to provide the deceased members with continuous happiness and well-being in the afterlife. For Vietnamese Catholics, this means that the living family members ensure a proper funeral and burial, which includes burying the deceased with objects they enjoyed in this world. Likewise, a picture or some other reminder of the deceased is placed in the family home as a reminder to continually pray for their soul. On the anniversary of the death, a Catholic Mass is offered, followed by a large gathering of family members for a banquet in memory of the deceased. Notes, money, and food are offered on the ancestor altar. The duties of remembering and maintaining the ritual usually fall to the children of the deceased.

The duties of ancestor veneration naturally require that families have children to continue the traditional practices. It is an attribute that affirms the Catholic teaching of procreation and the importance of building the family structures. Naturally, ancestor veneration shapes the requirement of filial piety—children must show respect to their living as well as to their deceased parents. Filial piety means respecting and obeying one's parents unconditionally while they are living and providing a proper funeral and remembrance/veneration of them when they die. This cultural tradition preceded but was formalized in the Confucian ideal of maintaining an orderly society through the five right relationships. These are the subject/ruler, father/son, older brother/younger brother, husband/wife, and friend/friend relationships. Respect is shown not only to immediate family members but to everyone in society. What these relationships accentuate is the Confucian ideal of deference to the elder or authority in society. This ideal may not have been formally learned in school, but for the Vietnamese family, it is handed down informally through the familial relationships. Many duties involved with this were then also translated into religious obligations for Vietnamese Catholics. This would later be codified through the parish community and Catholic schools.

Many catechetical books have weaved together ancestor veneration and filial piety with religious obligations and language. *Chon Dao Dan Giai* (*The True Religion Explained*) and *Hieu Kinh Cha Me* (*Filial Piety and the Respect of Parents*) enumerate believers' duties and practices toward God, authority figures, and their parents. Faithful Catholics are obligated to worship God with faith, trust, and love. Children are to show respect and gratitude toward their parents and others in authority. Filial piety falls under three aspects: custom, things related to the body, and things related to the soul. Obeying parents gives them recognition to children as representatives of God. If parents order their children to act in a way that is in opposition to God's law, they can renounce their duties. The children are to pay attention to both the material and spiritual needs of their parents. For example, when a parent is ill or unable to attend Mass, the children must make sure Communion is taken to them. Following these duties, the children will be rewarded in this life and the next. The consequence for ignoring these duties is shame placed on them and their family's reputation in this life and the next. Due to a strong sense of filial duty, Vietnamese Catholics often maintain a strong tradition of Catholic practices and devotion.

DEEP MARIAN DEVOTION

There is a strong devotion to the Blessed Virgin Mary within Vietnamese Catholicism, especially through the accounts of her apparitions. Two Marian apparitions occurred in Vietnam, one in La Vang (more popularly known) and the other at Tra Kieu. The account of Mary at La Vang in 1798 was associated with the Tay Son rebellion. The story has been passed down through several generations of Vietnamese Catholics. There are several different versions of the story told by Vietnamese Catholics and French missionaries, but all agree in reporting that Mary appeared to several people. The story describes how several Catholics chased from their village were gathered under a banyan tree to pray for protection against their attackers. As they huddled under the tree, a beautiful lady wearing a magnificent cloak appeared with the Infant Jesus in her arms. She heard their cry for help, and her message was that she would always help them in time of need. She appeared several more times, and news of her appearance spread throughout the villages.

The apparition did not immediately draw believers to La Vang, because the harsh terrain and continual persecution made the journey quite treacherous. Nonetheless, small pilgrimages to La Vang began in 1882. By 1901, with the dedication of a new church to Our Lady of La Vang, more pilgrims flocked there, with pilgrimages continuing today and numbering in the hundreds of thousands. It also draws Vietnamese from all over the world.

The apparition at Tra Kieu occurred during the time when the Vietnamese Catholic Church was afflicted with persecution by the reigning emperor Ham Nghi in 1885. A French missionary priest, Jean Bruyere, was surrounded by the emperor's army, which was attacking the whole parish community. While the young men and boys of the parish were out fighting against the attackers, Fr. Bruyere urged the others to place a statue of Mary on a table and recite the Rosary. The larger section of the emperor's army was held off for several days. They brought cannons to shoot at the church. The cannons missed the church, and a soldier reported seeing a lady dressed in white standing on top of the church. There is no way to validate these apparition stories, nor has the Vatican taken up the investigations. But Vietnamese Catholics do not hesitate to attribute Mary's miraculous intervention to their victory over their enemies. As with La Vang, a chapel was built in Tra Kieu in 1898, and pilgrimages have been organized since then.[22]

These apparitions contribute to the fact that Mary is supportive and protective of her children. Unlike the apparitions in Europe—especially at Lourdes and Fatima—where Mary's message was a message of conversion, in Vietnam, it was of protection and well-being. Mary's liberation of the persecuted believers creates the image of a Divine Mercy that speaks powerfully to Vietnamese Catholics who have been persecuted since missionary times. Even though these Marian apparitions have not been officially recognized by the Vatican, they continue to be a major influence on the lives of Vietnamese Catholics in Vietnam and around the world. These appearances capture a strong devotion of the Vietnamese people to a maternal spirit that has played a role in the history of Vietnam.

MARTYRDOM

It is estimated that between 130,000 and 300,000 Vietnamese Catholics died during the persecutions from 1625 to 1886. Between 1900 and 1909, the pope beatified ninety-two Catholics in Vietnam who had died in communitarian violence in the nineteenth century. Sixteen of them were missionaries (seven MEP and nine Spanish Dominicans), but seventy-six were Vietnamese, and they were the first ever to receive such an honor. Twenty-five more were beatified in 1951, and in 1988, Pope John Paul II canonized 117, including some well-known catechists such as Andrew Dung Lac, Phanxico Xavier Can, Vincent Diem, Phaolo Le Bao Tinh, Phero Nguyen Khac

---

22   Peter C. Phan, *Vietnamese-American Catholics* (New York/Mahway, NJ: Paulist Press, 2005), 115-116.

Tu, and Agnes Le Thi Thanh.[23] The beatifications and canonizations were the ultimate recognition of the struggles of the faithful believers. Catholics had long venerated those killed in religious violence, treating their relics as sacred objects and making the martyrs (*thanh tu dao*) figures of devotion. These martyrs stand as witnesses for a people who have struggled to define their place within a country that has endured much strife and unrest caused by external as well as internal forces. Nevertheless, the celebrations of these martyrs went through different phases.

Before 1925, the martyrs were often honored alongside Joan of Arc, usually around May 8, when she lifted the siege of Orleans, or May 30, her feast day. But in 1925, the newly appointed apostolic delegate to Vietnam decreed the first Sunday in September as a national day of mourning for Vietnam's martyrs.[24] The people were to be given notice by pastoral letters issued by the bishops with the schedule of the celebrations and brief biographies of the martyrs and accounts of their deaths. This fluctuation in dates, as well as waiting for the pastoral letters, created confusion and so failed to provide the honor that these martyrs needed. Lay Catholics raised the concern that since these martyrs are part of the Catholic family, they should be given filial respect as parents of the Vietnamese Catholic faith. A fixed date was given. Today the Vietnamese martyrs are celebrated on November 24 in the universal Catholic liturgical calendar. Catholics celebrate the canonization of these martyrs annually throughout Vietnam. The traditional practice of remembering the martyrs in the home country is brought to America, where large congregations gather to venerate and remember these martyrs as their ancestors in faith. These celebrations have also become an occasion for Vietnamese American Catholics to remember their home country while living out their faith in a new place. It is to this new place that we turn to understand the future of the Vietnamese American Catholics.

---

23 See *www.liendoanconggiao.net* for a full list and stories about the martyrs and their continual influence on the lives of Vietnamese Catholics today.
24 *Catholic Vietnam*, 133.

Future of Vietnamese American Catholics

The future of Vietnamese American Catholics is encouraging, especially given the large number of vocations to the priesthood and consecrated life. It is a sign that the community nurtures these vocations but also respects its religious leaders. But this is only part of the story of Vietnamese American Catholics. To look only at those vocations would skew the bigger picture of the whole Vietnamese American Catholic community. In this final section, attention will be given to three broad concerns: generational challenges, racism—the "model minority" dilemma, and other issues such as trauma due to the effects of war and the use of technology. Briefly examining these three broad areas will highlight both the religious and cultural complexities that affect Vietnamese American Catholics.

GENERATIONAL CHALLENGES

Like many previous immigrants, Vietnamese Americans face generational challenges as well as some challenges that are distinctive to them. The first generation, especially the elderly, consider filial piety as the key cultural variable in the functioning of the family. For many Vietnamese American parents, the continual practice of this filial piety becomes part of what they must instill in the second and subsequent generations. Vietnamese parents feel highly responsible for passing on this tradition in order to maintain their respect within their larger community and also within the immediate family.

The emphasis on the centrality of filial piety so important to Vietnamese American parents comes into conflict with the American idea that parents should have greater intimacy with their children. Vietnamese parents think that such intimacy undermines the children's respect for their parents. Second-generation Vietnamese, on the other hand, have absorbed the American value placed on intimacy and thus expect it of their first-generation parents. The conflict between the values of filial piety and family widens in America when parents need to work long hours and do not have time to teach their children the native culture and language. The distance also expands, because many parents work in isolated environments removed from "mainstream" American society and so remain highly ethnic and "un-Americanized." Such isolation contributes to the parents' already great difficulty in acquiring the English-language skills that the second-generation children typically feel more comfortable with. These factors add to an already formalized relationship between parents and children, creating a larger communication gap both linguistically and culturally.[25]

As intimacy wanes and the gaps widen between the generations, there is still the insatiable expectation that the first generation brings to bear on the second generation—repaying the sacrifice the parents made. Even though this may not be stated directly, the indirect expectation is that the burden is already instilled in the children and will remain as they continue to grow and develop their lives. In actuality, there really is no repaying of the sacrifice, but instead it underscores the tight bond required within a strong cultural adherence to filial piety.

From this relationship with their parents, the second generation struggles to understand the relationship between the parish and the family. They see their parents relying heavily on the parish, both for their own assimilation strategy and also for the children's faith formation, but ultimately these activities neglect the immediate family needs. The time spent in church activities adds to busy work and school schedules that already take away from the parent/child time together. Parents seize the opportunities offered by the parish of leadership roles in order to raise their social status, which is not easily raised in the first generation within the larger society. Moreover, some in the second generation believe that their parents and the

---

25   Linh Hoang, "The Faith and Practice of Asian American Catholics," *New Theology Review* 23:1 (February 2010: 48-57).

parish, fearing possible dishonor associated with open sharing, have socialized them to be silent about their family issues and pretend that everything is fine. They maintain a functional relationship within the family that may hide real-life issues and problems. The parish needs to also provide the second generation a place to make their own where they can express their needs.[26] This is done through the Vietnamese Eucharistic Youth Movement, which is getting wider attention.

Through church activities, the first-generation leaders incorporate the English-speaking second generation at any cost but also consistently exclude the second generation from leadership roles. The leadership positions that are held by the first generation are very important, because they sustain their own community while passing the faith on to the next generations. The leaders should be trained and also learn to share responsibilities so that all can understand the call to be disciples of Jesus. This issue is not unique to the Vietnamese Catholic community; it is part of the larger Church structure where leadership is not nurtured effectively among the young adults, but rather young leaders are made to wait their turn.

There are also differences in parish participation between the generations. Those differences can be gleaned from the following: first, the pastoral needs of people in their twenties differ from those of a group in their forties and fifties. Second, first-generation immigrants generally lack integration into American society and depend heavily on contact with others from their native country. In contrast, members of the second generation can choose from more organizational options. They generally feel more comfortable in American society and are not restricted to ethnic organizations. Third, there are differences in education and religious experiences that shape their expectations of the Church. The second generation is more likely to work toward a formal education or degree for a better understanding of their faith.

---

26   "The Faith and Practice of Asian American Catholics," 57.

Generally, some second-generation faithful are also taking the opportunity to obtain a theological or religious education. They are becoming more educated about their religion than their parents. This may be a reason why they are moving away from their parents' more devotional Catholicism. The tension between learned faith and pious devotion needs further examination. It is a tension that exists not only between the generations but within the larger Vietnamese American Catholic communities, and it extends to the larger American Catholic Church. The second generation will need to bring together the devotional faith of their first-generation parents and the education that they have earned in order, in time, to create a much more robust Catholic expression.

RACISM: "MODEL MINORITY" BUT "FOREVER FOREIGN"

The "model minority" applied to Asian Americans in general does not cover all ethnicities within the larger Asian American family. One way to understand the "model minority" is through academic achievement. For instance, Vietnamese do not fit neatly into the "model minority," because their academic achievement has lagged behind other Asian Americans such as Chinese, Koreans, and Japanese. While many Vietnamese have done well in school, there are a disproportionately higher percentage of dropouts from high school compared to other Asian Americans.[27]

The 2010 U.S. Census created an extensive study on the racial makeup of the United States. From this data, there is also information on the educational achievement of different ethnic groups. The data showed that adult Vietnamese Americans have lower educational achievements compared to other Asian Americans. Only 38 percent of Vietnamese Americans possess a high school diploma, and only 19.5 percent hold a bachelor's degree. These numbers place Vietnamese outside of the "Asian American" group (Chinese, Japanese, Koreans,

---

27   Bic Ngo and Stacey J. Lee, "Complicating the Image of Model Minority Success: A Review of Southeast Asian American Education," *Review of Educational Research* 77:4 (December, 2007): 415-453.

and Filipinos). Among Asian Americans, 42.7 percent hold a college degree, which is almost twice as high as white Americans.[28]

There are many studies about the achievements of Vietnamese students, especially since many overcame all odds as refugees to embrace the education afforded to them. There are very high-achieving Vietnamese, and they do deserve the accolades, but they are, unfortunately, only a small portion within the larger Vietnamese American population. It is a complicated portrait rather than a straight-line achievement story. On the one hand, Vietnamese are viewed as hardworking, high achievers. On the other hand, they are portrayed as high school dropouts, gang members, and welfare dependents. The experiences of Vietnamese Americans in U.S. schools and society are then reduced to the extreme, in which they usually end up on the negative side of the overall educational achievement of the Asian American discussion.

What is disturbing is that the studies of Vietnamese Americans' educational achievements do not look at those underachieving or neglected from the educational system in general. This is a concern, especially when the number of underachieving or struggling Vietnamese is at a much higher percentage than those who have captured the attention of the general population as part of the overachieving "model minority."[29]

Vietnamese cultural values are a vital factor in the educational success of Vietnamese American children. The successful adaption, as researchers have pointed out, is not due to Vietnamese willingness to adapt to American customs but rather to an adherence to traditional values and norms instilled by their parents. The most successful Vietnamese youth are those who adhere to family and community values and do not become "too American." The educational achievement is a collective affair, where the children along with their parents and the extended family encourage and promote education.[30]

28   http://www.census.gov/prod/cen2010/briefs/c2010br-11.pdf p. 2.
29   "Complicating the Image of Model Minority Success," 415-453.
30   "Complicating the Image of Model Minority Success," 415-453.

The evidence of struggle needs to be highlighted, especially when tensions and problems are not addressed. A significant number of Vietnamese youth are estranged from American culture, alienated from school, and pushed into gangs. Although Vietnamese students believe their parents are interested in their education and success, they also report that their parents do not attend school functions to meet their teachers or participate in school activities. Substantial anecdotal evidence points to delinquency as an issue of growing significance among younger-generation Vietnamese. Although Vietnamese youths have made remarkable academic achievements, they have also showed relatively high rates of juvenile delinquency and youth gang involvement.[31]

According to sociologists Min Zhou and Carl Bankston III, the highest rates of delinquency occur within the second generation. These low-achieving, delinquent youth are described as having lost their culture. This is coupled with the idea that they have become too Americanized and disconnected from co-ethnic networks. In addition, intergenerational conflict and loss of parental authority are said to put youth at risk for delinquent behavior. Another explanation includes the shift in the power relations between adults and youth when the youth take over adult roles, such as paying bills and dealing with outside authorities, because their English-language skills are much stronger.

Vietnamese students must juggle responsibilities in the home with household chores and also act as translators and cultural brokers for parents and other relatives. The long work hours of parents leave no time to support the children's homework, attend to how children are spending their free time, or address the children's problems. Vietnamese students who have difficulties in school can trace it back to those rooted problems at home.

The collective educational pursuits create enormous pressure for Vietnamese students to do well in school. For Vietnamese children, their future as well as the future of other family members hinges on their success.

---

31 Min Zhou and Carl Bankston III, *Growing Up American: How Vietnamese Children Adapt to Life in the United States* (New York: Russell Sage Foundation, 1998), 185-186.

Although research on Vietnamese students' education stresses the influence of family, community, and culture on student achievement, some research points to the role schools play in student achievement. Many schools are not equipped to teach language to minority students. Some are placed in classes that exceed their English proficiency. When Vietnamese children do poorly as a result of the placement, they tend to become embarrassed, lose confidence, and become truant and drop out. Some researchers point to acts of racism as affecting the education of Vietnamese students.[32]

In a similar way, where schools play a role in student achievement, the Church plays a role in maintaining the faithful's participation. Parishes must adapt to include and maintain the loyalty of believers. The second and subsequent generation must be pulled into roles in the parish that are not limited to singing in the choir or lectoring at Mass. Rather, they must be called into leadership roles and social justice activities that will sustain them. These will give them responsibility as well as recognition for their contribution to the wider faith community.

OTHER ISSUES: TRAUMA AND TECHNOLOGY

One of the issues that many refugees face is the trauma of being displaced and the stress of leaving a homeland. This can either be diagnosed clinically as post-traumatic stress disorder, in which case counseling would be necessary, or as trauma in the sense of enduring the stress of fleeing and resettling. In either case, scant attention was given to many Vietnamese refugees who fled during the late 1970s to 1990s. The issue of trauma among refugees of war and persecution was not discussed among the refugee population in the early days of resettlement; however, the trauma of fleeing their country does not disappear.

Many Vietnamese are not familiar with psychological counseling, since it was not practiced in Vietnam, and therefore they are less

---

32   "Complicating the Image of Model Minority Success," 415-453.

likely to seek out counseling when needed. Eventually, many refugees accepted the fact that they needed help outside of the family structure to deal with the trauma of resettlement. Thus, the demand for counselors rose among the refugee population, but there were not enough Vietnamese-speaking counselors to help those in most need. In response to the need, places were created to provide safe zones, even if they were not run by professional counselors. These provided a place for the refugees to express their anxieties, depression, and trauma. This became an excellent opportunity for the Church to provide such resources. This has been done in the early resettlement, but ongoing follow-up is still needed. Though psychological counseling is an area that is gaining attention among Vietnamese Americans, it is still not highly utilized. It is an area that the second and subsequent generations will use more than the first generation.[33]

Coupled with this concern about trauma is concern about the actions that result from it, especially suicide. There is no accurate data on the rate of suicide in general in the United States, due to many factors, including the stigma associated with suicide. There is mounting evidence that the rate is growing among Asian and Pacific Islander immigrant and refugee communities. This is a cultural and pastoral concern that the Vietnamese Catholic community can bring to discussion.

The last area of concern is about the use of technology, which can operate as a means to bridge the gap between the first and second generations. The second and subsequent generations are growing up and maturing in a society that moves much faster with the help of the Internet. The transmission of information, news, and knowledge flashes quickly. They are able to receive this information but may lack thoughtful reflection on how to process it. The community will need to respond to this by providing awareness to its members about best practices on the Internet.

---

33   Nazli Kibria, *Family Tightrope: The Changing Lives of Vietnamese Americans* (Princeton, NJ: Princeton University Press, 1993).

The Internet has provided better connections with the home country of Vietnam, and the first generation can now maintain closer contact with their immediate relatives. The use of social media has also drawn first- and second-generation Vietnamese closer, since it provides for communication and also a medium to learn about one another. But this also means that the first generation needs to learn the technology in which the second and subsequent generations have become so well versed. Vietnamese parents should learn to utilize technology—e-mail, Internet, websites, blogs, etc.—to keep up with their children's progress in school and also socially. They can maintain a connection even if they live far away from one another. The use of technology will also be important as the different generations continue to learn and improve their faith practices within the Church. This becomes an opportunity where Church leaders can tap into the resources that technology will provide.

Conclusion

The future for Vietnamese American Catholics is quite encouraging with the growing number of vocations, national parishes, and visible leaders. The tight-knit communities and parishes continue to grow together in faith and support youth organizations that work to encourage living faith-filled lives. They are an inspiration and encouragement to the larger American Church that has experienced a decline in weekly attendance as well as dwindling numbers in priestly and religious vocations. Vietnamese American Catholics will continue to participate as long as there are places and people who will help support them, provide for their needs, and encourage them in the faith.

But there are a couple of concerns. First, as Vietnamese Catholics continue to create a place in America, they will also face problems similar to previous immigrant groups. Many first-generation Vietnamese lament the fact that the second and subsequent generations do not participate widely in the Church. Participation is strongest among communities and parishes that have strong youth organizations such as the Eucharistic Youth Movement. These should be encouraged and given priority through paid staffing, since they are often currently run by volunteers.

Second, even though vocations are strong, Vietnamese Catholics do not have a large representation among the higher leadership positions in the Church, especially as bishops or superiors of religious communities. Leadership should be encouraged and nurtured in order to serve the vibrant lay communities. The priests and religious who are already involved should also be invited and encouraged to serve in leadership positions. Many have vast experiences in the Church and can contribute more to the wider Church as well as Vietnamese American Catholic communities.

Third, Vietnamese American Catholic communities should consider what type of church model they want to maintain. Traditionally, Vietnamese Catholics have worked from an institutional top-down model. While in Vietnam, this model served the community well. But in the United States, where many parishes are staffed by one priest or none at all, the laity has maintained the functioning of the parish. They are the backbone of these communities. Indirectly, Vietnamese American Catholics are utilizing a more collaborative parish model that gives voice to their abilities. This should be encouraged and continue to develop, especially in areas where it is not already happening. This will be encouraging also for younger Catholics, as they can take up leadership positions in their respective communities and parishes. The younger generations need to be encouraged and supported in their involvement.

Finally, Vietnamese American Catholics have demonstrated courageously that challenges become an opportunity to create a new life through the support of God. They have overcome the trauma of fleeing their war-torn country to establish a place in the United States. Their presence is noted in various communities on both the East and West Coasts of the United States as well as in other major metropolitan areas. The resettling process provided many the opportunities to recreate a new life and also created a renewed sense of Church grounded in their tradition. Their strong duty to family, both living and deceased, deep devotion to Mary, and espousal of the tradition of the Catholic faith sustain their place in an American Catholic Church that continues to be a living witness to the gospel message of Jesus Christ.

Bibliography

Aguilar-San Juan, Karin. *Little Saigons: Staying Vietnamese in America.* Minneapolis & London: University of Minnesota Press, 2009.

Bankston III, Carl L. "Vietnamese-American Catholicism: Transplanted and Flourishing." *U.S. Catholic Historian* 18:1 (Winter 2000): 36-53.

Duiker, William J. *Ho Chi Minh: A Life.* New York: Hyperion, 2000.

Freeman, James M. *Changing Identities: Vietnamese Americans, 1975-1995.* Boston, MA: Allyn and Bacon, 1995.

Haines, David W., ed. *Refugees as Immigrants: Cambodians, Laotians, and Vietnamese in America.* Totow, NJ: Rowman & Littlefield Publishers, Inc., 1989.

Hein, Jeremy. *From Vietnam, Laos, and Cambodia: A Refugee Experience in the United States.* New York: Twayne Publishers, 1995.

Hoang, Linh. "The Faith and Practice of Asian American Catholics." *New Theology Review* 23:1 (February 2010): pp. 48-57.

Huon, Phan Phat. *History of the Catholic Church in Vietnam.* Long Beach, CA: Cuu The Tung Thu, 2000.

Keith, Charles. *Catholic Vietnam: A Church from Empire to Nation.* Berkeley & Los Angeles: University of California Press, 2012.

_____. "Annam Uplifted: The First Vietnamese Catholic Bishops and the Birth of a National Church, 1919-1945." *Journal of Vietnamese Studies* 3:2 (Summer 2008): 128-171.

Kibria, Nazli. *Family Tightrope: The Changing Lives of Vietnamese Americans.* Princeton, NJ: Princeton University Press, 1993.

Nash, Jesse W. *Vietnamese Catholicism.* Harvey, LA: Art Review Press, 1992.

Ngo, Bic, and Stacey J. Lee. "Complicating the Image of Model Minority Success: A Review of Southeast Asian American Education." *Review of Educational Research* 77:4 (December 2007): 415-453.

Phan, Peter C. *Vietnamese-American Catholics.* New York/Mahway, NJ: Paulist Press, 2005.

_____. *Mission and Catechesis: Alexandre de Rhodes and Inculturation in Seventeenth-Century Vietnam.* Maryknoll, NY: Orbis Books, 1998.

_____. "Vietnamese Catholics in the United States: Christian Identity Between the Old and the New." *U.S. Catholic Historian* 18/1 (Winter 2000): 19-35.

Zhou, Min and Carl J. Bankston III. *Growing Up American: How Vietnamese Children Adapt to Life in the United States.* New York: Russell Sage Foundation, 1998.